VIA FOLIOS 107

THE HERO ENKIDU

THE HERO ENKIDU

An Epic

LEWIS TURCO

BORDIGHERA PRESS

Library of Congress Control Number: 2015936729

Printed in the United States.

Published by
BORDIGHERA PRESS
John D. Calandra Italian American Institute
25 W. 43rd Street, 17th Floor
New York, NY 10036

VIA Folios 107
ISBN 978–1–59954–098–6

DEDICATION

For Jean

who chose to spend her life with me, with love and gratitude,
and in memory of my parents,

Luigi Turco

whose Sicilian-Middle-Eastern heritage is embodied in his
family name and in the text of this story, and

May Laura Putnam

whose Danish-English heritage is embodied in the form in
which this text is written.

ACKNOWLEDGMENTS

The Foreword, the Prologue, and "Canto I: Nimrod and Lilitu" of *The Hero Enkidu* originally appeared on-line in *Per Contra,* as did the discussion in the Afterword, of "The Gawain Poet."

"Canto IV: The Return of Enkidu," appeared on-line in *Radius.*

"The City's Mask" was published in *Quartet,* No. 8, 1964.

"The Green Knight and the White" appeared in the print periodical *Measure* in 2015.

TABLE OF CONTENTS

Introduction by Michael Palma 13

Foreword 17

Prologue 19

Canto I: Nimrod and Lilitu 21

Canto II: Erech 27

Canto III: The Betrayal of Lilitu 37

Canto IV: The Return of Enkidu 43

Canto V: The Forest of Humbaba 49

Canto VI: Ishtar's Proposal 57

Canto VII: The Bull of Heaven 65

Canto VIII: The Death of Enkidu 71

Epilogue 75

Afterword 81

INTRODUCTION

Over the long course of human history, *The Epic of Gilgamesh* has undergone one of the strangest odysseys of any work of literature. Preserved on twelve clay tablets in the extensive library of the ruler Ashurbanipal in the city of Nineveh, it must have exerted a powerful influence over the culture of the ancient Near East. In the character of Utnapishtim, it has direct links to the biblical story of Noah and the Flood. Its two halves, focusing respectively on warlike exploits and an arduous quest, may very well have been remote predecessors of the Homeric epics. And yet, after the fall of Nineveh in 612 B.C., *Gilgamesh* lay buried beneath the desert sands, forgotten for nearly two and a half millennia until the library was unearthed in December 1853. Its rediscovery sparked excitement in the English-speaking world largely because of the biblical parallels, as exemplified in George Smith's *The Chaldean Account of Genesis* (1875). Since then, emphasis has fallen largely upon the literary value of the work, with fine retellings done by a number of distinguished writers, including William Ellery Leonard, Nigel Dennis, and David Ferry.

In addition to such serious efforts, however, sports and mutants abound, and from almost the beginning the adventures of *Gilgamesh* in the English language have been a very long, strange trip indeed. As early as 1884 there appeared Leonidas Le Cenci Hamilton's *Ishtar and Izdubar, The Epic of Babylon,* a two-hundred-page poem in heroic couplets with interspersed lyrics that, issues of quality aside, bears about the same relationship to its source that *Othello* does to Cinthio's *Un Capitano Moro.* Beyond other poetic versions of greatly varying accomplishment, *Gilgamesh* has inspired (or, at the very least, lent its title character's name to) two science-fiction novels by Robert Silverberg, at least five operas, and assorted comic books and video games. In all this mass of material, Enkidu, the faithful companion and in some respects savior of Gilgamesh, retains his secondary status, when he appears at all. But now, with Lewis Turco's *The Hero Enkidu,* his four-thousand-year stint in the wings is over, and he steps out onto center stage at last.

In the original epic, Gilgamesh is shocked to discover that Utnapishtim is just lolling about through eternity, making little or no use of his divine gift of immortality. Lewis Turco, on the other hand, appears to have combined the longevity of Utnapishtim with the energy and industry of Gilgamesh: once seized with inspiration, he wrote *The Hero Enkidu* at white heat in his eightieth year. The inspiration itself is of the kind that, once someone has come up with it, makes us wonder why no one ever thought of it before, because in a number of ways Enkidu is a more interesting and attractive figure than Gilgamesh. The story of Enkidu's creation and especially of his seduction away from his life among the beasts is one of the most striking parts of the original epic. Gilgamesh is arrogant — exercising *droit de seigneur* and otherwise making himself as obnoxious as possible to his subjects — and as petulant as Achilles, until his energies are refocused by the coming of Enkidu, who appears manly and composed throughout (just as he is in *The Hero Enkidu,* including those parts of it, such as the third canto, that are wholly of Turco's invention). It is Enkidu who persuades Gilgamesh not to give in to pity but instead to complete his mission and slay the monster Humbaba. Even as he is dying and curses the temple prostitute for having indirectly contributed to his untimely death, Enkidu is quickly persuaded that it was better to have lived a short but human life than the protracted, meaningless existence of an animal.

Throughout, *The Hero Enkidu* moves with a swiftness and strength that are wholly appropriate to the adventures it recounts and the character of the protagonist. A particular case in point occurs in Canto VI, in a seventy-line speech in which Enkidu rejects the marriage proposal of the goddess Ishtar, recounting the unfortunate fates of all those who have been unlucky enough to excite her interest, a passage that surpasses the original in its vigor and inventiveness. This is owing in no small part to the form that Turco, with instincts honed by a lifetime of poetic practice, has chosen for the poem. The author of *The Book of Forms* and of *Ancient Music,* a collection of lyrics inspired by medieval Welsh and English poems, has here employed the alliterative hemistich and caesura of Anglo-Saxon verse combined with the "bob-and-wheel," the five-line rhyming tag that ends each stanza of the fourteenth-century English masterpiece *Sir Gawain and the Green Knight.* By writing in a form not used in the ancient epic, Turco escapes a sedulous adherence to his source and frees his imagination to create some haunting effects, as in this passage from Canto III:

> In March Enkidu
> > > lost his dream,
> Began to waken.
> > > The wild wind
> Roared at the door,
> > > > rattled the jambs —
> He lifted his lids
> > > > to squint at light
> Falling across
> > > the frosty sill
> Onto the floor
> > > > where chill tiles
> > > > > > challenged him
> > > > To step into the day
> > > > > Where sunshine and the grim
> > > > > Mists of morning lay
> > > > > > In shades both bright and dim.

As time flew
          it turned the tiles
From bone white
           to warm green.
Flowers bloomed
           under the sill,
Soothed by the sun,
           stroked by the wind
That wandered whispering
           in the June light
That daily rose
           and fell through the panes.
               Out of the deep
          Dark the hero would awaken
           From his sound sleep
          And a rest well taken
           To daylight's castle-keep.

In the wildwood
          beyond his panes
The falcons fledged.
           Leaves shed tiles
On the forest floor
          of shadow and light
Until at last
          a darker green
Began to shimmer
          in a sharper wind
And sere leaves
          sailed past the sill
             like pennants of a boat.
          Ripples broke the glass
           Of blue that used to float
          And reflect on clouds that pass
           Over the tower's moat.

In this little book Lewis Turco has achieved a great deal. He has told a fast-moving, vivid, and compelling story. He has struck a blow of liberation for all the great sidekicks, the Sancho Panzas and Dr. Watsons. And, in a manner reminiscent of the author of *Sir Gawain*, whose poem looked back to *Beowulf* as it stood on the threshold of the splendid tradition of English verse, he has taken the oldest story in the world and made it into the newest.

— Michael Palma

FOREWORD

Those who are interested in such things as epics are likely to know that *The Epic of Gilgamesh* "is, perhaps, the oldest written story on Earth. It comes to us from Ancient Sumeria, and was originally written on 12 clay tablets in cuneiform script," the Academy for Ancient Texts avers on its Web page. "It is about the adventures of the historical King of Uruk [Erech, modern Iraq] (somewhere between 2750 and 2500 BCE)." In fact, however, it is an amalgamation of two stories, the older having to do with the adventures of a most likely mythological person named "Enkidu," and the second about an ancient King of Erech.

Over the course of no one knows how many centuries, the two tales of Enkidu and *Gilgamesh* became intertwined and it is in this form that *Gilgamesh* has come down to us in various versions and languages. To blend the earlier tale of Enkidu with the later doings of *Gilgamesh*, apparently in order to ascribe to the latter many of the feats of the former, the pair came to be seen as in some essential ways twins, even to the point where they look alike, for the King is a bit taller, it seems, and his close companion Enkidu is broader.

What I have attempted to do here is to cut away from the *Gilgamesh* epic those actions and events that can quite clearly be ascribed to the older Enkidu and to write his own tale in the manner of the author of the anonymous Medieval epic titled *Gawain and the Green Knight,* that is to say, in cantos of the strong-stress metric line called Anglo-Saxon prosody with appended five-line accentual-syllabic metrical tails called "bobs-and-wheels."

I do not claim to have restored the Enkidu epic, nor am I writing history: I am still writing fiction, like the original author(s), and I could not absolutely separate *Gilgamesh* and his companion. What I do claim is that I have given back to Enkidu what pretty clearly is his tale, and I hope I have written it in a comprehensible and interesting way for modern audiences.

My sources are few and select. I used primarily *An Old Babylonian Version of the Gilgamesh Epic,* etc., by Morris Jastrow, Jr., and Albert T. Clay, New Haven: Yale, 1920, supplemented by "Monsters from Mesopotamia," an illustrated essay by Robert Lebling, in my favorite periodical of many years' standing, *Saudi Aramco World,* Vol. 63, No. 4, July-August 2012, which gave me the idea for my endeavor, the first little bit of which was a sestina in Anglo-Saxon prosody with bobs and wheels added titled, "The Green Knight and the White" which appeared in a print journal (see Acknowledgments) in 2015 and which is appended to this text in the Afterword.

Lewis Turco
October 14, 2013

PROLOGUE

From a clump of clay
                Aruru created
The hero Enkidu,
            molded him
In the image of Anu,
                God of the Sky,
Free as a fawn
              in the forest of cedars,
Noble offspring
             of the host of Ninib.
She threw him into
              an open meadow
Among the beasts
             where he would be
One of them,
          fully feral,
Hirsute and bearded
              like the awns of barley,
Built to be
        a mighty warrior.
Enkidu knew
           neither folk nor land,
But like the gazelles
             browsed on herbs,
Drank his fill,
          delighting his heart
                   at the flowing spring,
            bathing in its balm,
              beneath the cedars sleeping
            in dreamless dark and calm
             where there is no weeping.

CANTO I: NIMROD AND LILITU

Nimrod entered
             the fertile forest
And found the traps
                that he had dug
Had all been filled
                with soil and scrub;
That all the springes
                he had set
Had been sprung,
                had trapped no game.
He wondered who
                it was had dealt
So meanly with
                his weal and fare —
Then he saw
                the wolf-man
Hairy and naked
                among the herds
Like one of them,
                lion-strong,
Panther-quick,
                quiet afoot!
Nimrod stood
                to draw his bow,
But with a roar
                Enkidu saw him,
Began to attack,
                wild as a werewolf,
But when he saw
                the hairless creature
Standing before him
                Enkidu stopped,
To stare, astonished,
                at this wonder,
                                then stood in sorrow,
                in agony and woe
                    to see this man aglow
                    with manliness as though
                        he were godlike crown to toe.

Enkidu knew
              now he was naked
And Nimrod clothed.
                        He understood
And cried aloud
              at his condition,
Compared it with
                  Nimrod's grace.
Never had he
              known his shame
Before this day,
                  only the brutish
Beasts of woodland
                    and savannah.
He paused a moment
                      then turned and ran.
Nimrod could not
                  overtake him,
Returned instead
                  upon his steed
Safely home
              to his sire Cush,
Grandson of Noah,
                    the Flood's sailor
And survivor.
                  When he arrived
He said, "Father,
                I have found
What it was
              that tore my nets
And foiled me there
                    in the cedar forest —
The greatest beast
                  beneath the sun;
                          he looks much like a man,
                    but moves upon four feet
                        and covers a greater span
                  than the cheetah, quick and fleet,
                    or the prideful lion can.

Cush replied,
              "Go, my son,
Take with you
              a courtesan,

She who is best,
                    most beautiful
Among the hetaera
                    who are for hire.
Return to the woodland
                    and wait for him
To appear again
                    among the herds
Who gather to drink
                    at the fluid spring.
When he comes forth
                    to slake his thirst
She must shed
                    her mantle to show
Her beauteous body.
                    He shall espy her
Be entranced,
                    approach and embrace her.
                              When he does
                    the beasts shall all forsake him,
                        both the bucks and ewes,
                    those that fly and swim —
                    if he calls, all will refuse."

Nimrod procured
                    the prostitute
Cush had advised:
                    Lilitu
Was her name.
                    He ventured forth
With her to return
                    to his traps and woods.
Three days they wended
                    their way abroad,
Until at last
                    they found the forest,
Waited in the cedars'
                    silence and shade.
A pair of days
                    passed till the beasts
Came to slake
                    their thirst at the spring,
And with them Enkidu
                    to delight his heart

With laving water.
                    There the doxy
Beheld the lusty
                    desert-monster.
"He is the one,
                    my bountiful beauty,"
Nimrod said.
                    "Show him your comeliness,
That loveliness
                    which he may possess.
Reveal your body
                    in all its glory,
Let him be ravished
                    when his eyes' arrows
Fall upon you.
                    Free your mantle
From your flesh;
                    ply him with ploys
And the wiles of women.
                         Let him clasp you
To his breast."
                    The girl was shameless.
She loosened her mantle.
                         Enkidu came
Straightway to clasp her,
                    to ravish her.
He took her there
                    in rapture rare.
The sweet Lilitu
                    lay laughing,
Kissed his face
                    and fondled him;
Enkidu gladly
                    welcomed her kindness,
Admired her garb,
                    her glorious tresses,
Faultless features
                    and radiant hue.
Gladness arose
                    out of his heart.
Lilitu shaved
                    Enkidu's body,
Braided his beard
                    and combed his hair.

Again and again they mated,
six days and a final night,
until the lust was sated
in him. His herds took flight —
there were no beasts that waited.

From the depths of dream
Enkidu awakened,
Fought his way
from the fens of slumber,
Rose fleetly
to attend his fate
In ecstasies
of blissful song.

"Handsome Enkidu,
like a god are you!
Why with the cattle
do you roam?
Come, arise
from this cursed forest
And we will journey
to walled Erech."
Enkidu had lost
his innocence,
Achieved the growth
of his true manhood,
Broadened his wisdom.
He sat at the feet
Of this woman who scanned
his face and eyes.
"Up!" she said, "up!
Away to Erech
To the temple of Anu,
the altar of Ishtar!
There you shall meet
your mirror-man,
Gilgamesh
who rules like an aurochs.
I will summon him,
challenge him boldly,
Cry through Erech,
'Here is he
Who is mighty also,
who will alter fate,

Born in the desert.
                              His vigor is greatest.'
Enkidu, come!
                    Erech is waiting
Where people array
                              themselves in attire
Gay and festive,
                    each day a revel,
The eunuch priests
                         clash their cymbals,
Dancing houris
                    are gleeful and wanton —
They keep the nobles
                         out of their divans!
Come, Enkidu,
                    love life fully,
Taste its sweets,
                    Erech awaits
As does its ruler,
                    great Gilgamesh,
                              your mirror image,
                         mightiest warrior living,
                              full of pride and courage,
                         yet generous and giving.
                              No longer need you forage."

CANTO II: ERECH

On their trek to Erech
                    Lilitu told
Enkidu the tale
                    of the city's founding:
"In the second age
                    Isildur carried
Out of the ruins
                    of golden Númenor
A great globe
                    made of stone.
Upon the stone
                    he etched an oath
And caused the great
                    King of the Mountains
To place his hand
                    upon the rock
And swear that he
                    would bear fealty,
To Isildur's lineage
                    and to Erech when
Its temple and walls
                    were raised upon
The crown of the hill.
                    Isildur built
A ziggurat then,
                    the White Temple,
And worshipped
                    there Anu and Inanna,
Sky sovereigns.
                    But when the time
Came at last
                    to honor their oath,
The Men of the Mountains
                    would not fight
The wizard Sargon,
                    for they had worshipped
Him erewhile
                    in the Dark Years.
Isildur cursed them,
                    swore that they

Would never rest
                till they had fulfilled
Their ancient oath.
                    Erech was desolate
When the Third Age
                came to an end
Because the Terror
                of the Sleepless Dead
Lay on the hill
              and the White Temple.
Then Aragorn came,
                arrived in Erech
To hold the army
             of the undead
To their sworn word.
                  They obeyed this time
And helped Aragorn
                defeat the Corsairs
Of Umbar at Pelargir.
                After the battle
Aragorn released
             the ghostly host
From their curse
             and they went to rest.
                        At last the mountain men
                    were given their surcease.
                      They could not remember when
                  they last had lived in peace.
                    They would not rise again."

Enkidu and
             Lilitu traveled
Through the desert
              long leagues
Until at last
            they saw the walls
That Gilgamesh
              not long since
Had built about
            the metropolis.
Enkidu marveled
             at their height
And at the strength
              such walls displayed.

"Gilgamesh
                must be mighty!"
He exclaimed.
                "Mighty indeed,"
Agreed his harlot.
                        "He is the fifth
Lord of the founding
                        dynastic line.
He will reign
                a hundred years
And more, the oracles
                        and seers predict.
His father's name
                was Lugalbanda,
His mother, the goddess
                        Rimat Ninsun;
Thus Gilgamesh
                is a demigod,
His strength the strength
                        of a thousand lions.
He built this wall
                to defend his capital,
But he has erected
                many things.
He and his son,
                Urlugal,

In Tummal rebuilt
                the sanctuary
Of the goddess Ninlil,
                Lady of the Field
And Lady of the Wind,
                who was my mother."
                                Enkidu stopped to stare
                                At Lilitu, his mate.
                        He stood astonished there,
                                considering his fate
                        and whither he should fare.

"You had not
                told me that,"
Enkidu said.
                "You did not ask,"
Answered Lilitu.

               "Why did one
As powerful
          as you come
To capture me?"
               "Who but a temptress
Could capture
          you, Enkidu?"
The companions stood
               in contemplation
Of one-another
          there before
The walls of Erech.
               Lilitu broke
The silence. "And who
               but one like me
Might teach you to speak?
               You lived among
The herds of the field,
            the beasts in the cedars
That covered the hills."
               "Teach me to speak?"
Again Enkidu
          was stunned and astonished.
"Indeed," said Lilitu,
            "when did you
First speak
          rather than snarl
And howl like the wolf
             you used to be?"
Enkidu lost
          himself in thought.
"When I awoke
            from sleep beside you
And you shaved my body."
               Lilitu nodded.
                    "I cast a spell
              upon you as you slept
                where you had used to dwell.
              You had become adept
               while in our sylvan dell.

"Come you now,
          my dear Enkidu,
Let us enter

          into Erech
To meet the lord
              of the land. He awaits
Our arrival
          most eagerly.
He knows of you
             and of your prowess,
For he has dreamt
            of your coming.
He is curious to meet
               his soul-brother,
The twin that fate
             has made for him,
The twin that he
          has never seen."

"How do I
          resemble Gilgamesh?"

"He is a little
          taller, perhaps,
But not so husky,"
            Lilitu replied.
"Otherwise there is
             but little distinction."
And as she spoke
          the great gates
Of Erech swung
          wide before them.
Gilgamesh stood
          among his panoply
Of warriors and courtiers.
               Lilitu bowed,
But Enkidu stood
          and gaped at the vision,
                  for he had never seen
           a sight like this before.
            It was a noble scene —
          he stood beside his whore
            and watched the court convene.

Gilgamesh
          spoke to them.
"Who art thou

who does not bow
before the master
                    of the city of Erech?"
Enkidu was struck
                    to a pillar of stone
For a moment,
                    then he fell
Upon his knees
                    before the monarch.
"Rise, Enkidu,
            I recognize
My friend and brother.
                    I was forewarned
That you would come.
                    I dreamt of you,
Told my mother,
                    Ninsun, my dream,
Which she deciphered
                    for my understanding."

Enkidu arose
            in wonderment.
"You dreamt of me,
                    my lord and master?"

"Not 'master,' Enkidu,
                    friend and brother.
'O my mother,'
            I said to her,
'A vision came
            to me by night.
I beheld the stars
            when suddenly
It seemed that Anu
                    himself fell
Down upon
            my shoulders. Although
I heaved him off
                    he was too heavy,
Stronger than I.
                    Although his grapple
Loosened somewhat
                    I could not shake
Him from my body.
                    The folk of Erech

Stood all about,
                    the artisans pressing
Him from behind.
                    Meanwhile, the heroes,
My own companions!
                              kissed his feet
As though he were
                    my peer and equal.
Then even I
            stood and embraced him
                                    almost as though
                    he were more than friend,
                          nothing like a foe,
                    more like a godsend
                              dropped on us here below.

"Ninsun said,
                    'The stars of heaven
Were all
            of your companions.
That which you thought
                        was Anu who fell
Upon your shoulders
                        was Enkidu, the twin
Of your very soul,
                    he whose strength
Is greater than any
                    the length and breadth
Of this land or other,
                    like Anu's own.'
                                    Thus I looked ahead
                    to this glorious moment gladly,
                        and all my worries fled,
                        for I need an ally badly --
                        now I need no longer dread."

Enkidu was welcomed
                        into Erech
Together with
                the witch Lilitu,
His companion

                and his mate.

They were treated as though
                         they were royal,
Even the hetaera,
                  though everyone
Knew that she
              was a night-walker.

Even though
            Gilgamesh
Had declared
             Enkidu his brother,
The master of Erech
                    was smitten. He coveted
This beauteous woman
                     where she lay
Among pillows
              strewn for the love-rites.
When night had fallen
                      Gilgamesh came
To sleep with her
                  and give her delight.
But he was blocked
                   by his friend Enkidu.
Enraged, Gilgamesh
                   rushed to attack him
Where he guarded the door.
                           They grappled like lions,
They snorted and roared,
                         shattered the threshold.
The walls of the palace
                        quivered as did
At last the legs
                 of the great Gilgamesh —
They bent beneath
                  the strength of the wolf-man
And he surrendered.
                    When he had to kneel
Upon the ground,
                 his ardor abated
As did his fury.
                 Enkidu said,
"Truly your mother
                   bore you as one,
And one only,

    the choicest steed
Of the stables.
    Ninsun exalted
Your head above heroes
     and Enlil endowed
You with the kingship
     above other men."
       "We are brothers now,
     You have title to the whore.
    You have won the laurel bough,"
     The King of Erech swore,
    "You need no longer bow."

CANTO III: THE BETRAYAL OF LILITU

Enkidu slept
          the sleep of the dead
In his love-bed
          beside Lilitu,
For before he closed
          the lids of his eyes
She gave him a potion
          that brought dreams
To the werewolf she
          had made a man.
One night
          Enkidu forgot
To imbibe the elixir
          and he awoke
At midnight to find
          Lilitu gone —
No longer was she
          beside him there
Among the pillows
          of Paradise.
Remembering his fight
          with Gilgamesh,
Enkidu crept
          into the hall
Where the king slept —
          Lilitu
Was not there.
          Enkidu raged
To think that Lilitu
          had betrayed him.
The moon was full
          in the night's heavens
When Enkidu howled
          beneath its beams.
He dropped again
          to all four feet
As he had erstwhile
          done in the forest,

Before he became
                    a human male.
His sense of smell
                    was keen as ever,
So he followed Lilitu's
                    scented trail.
At last he found her
                    in a crypt of ghouls
Consorting with them
                    and drinking the blood
Of infants from bowls
                    made of skulls.
Enkidu entered
                trembling with fury
And with disgust.
                    He called aloud
In the voice of a lion,
                    "Who are you
Who gather here
                    to engage in the rites
Of the gods of Evil?"
                    One stood forth
To face the Hero.
                "Seven are we
Who know no care.
                    We grind the earth
Like wheat; we neither
                    know nor show
Mercy to any.
                We rave against
Mortal mankind —
                    we spill its blood
Like storms of rain;
                    we drink from their veins
That turn dry as a wadi.
                        Lilitu is patroness
Of the Seven Spirits.
                    We crawl over Earth
Or travel with storms,
                    wind-demons,
Goblins and ghouls."
                    With one mighty
Thrust Endkidu
                brushed the spirits

Into the wind,
        and then he stood
Staring at
        Lilitu the vampire.

She looked at him
        with eyes of fire.
"I am not your kine,
        Enkidu my love.
My soul is mine
        as is my body.
I do with it
        as I please; I go
Whereever I go
        whenever I wish.
You have no rights
        to me or mine.
Why did you banish
        my Seven Spirits?"

Enkidu said nothing,
        he merely turned
And hastened away.
        He had to find
A place to stay
        and be alone
To deal with such   immense betrayal.
           He traveled far
       Until he found a tower
        Where he might lick this scar,
        Where he might brood and cower
        Beneath his evil star.

In March Enkidu
        lost his dream,
Began to waken.
        The wild wind
Roared at the door,
        rattled the jambs —
He lifted his lids
        to squint at light
Falling across
        the frosty sill

Onto the floor
        where chill tiles
                challenged him
      To step into the day
           Where sunshine and the grim
        Mists of morning lay
            In shades both bright and dim.

As time flew
        it turned the tiles
From bone white
           to warm green.
Flowers bloomed
          under the sill,
Soothed by the sun,
             stroked by the wind
That wandered whispering
               in the June light
That daily rose
        and fell through the panes.
                    Out of the deep
          Dark the hero would awaken
           From his sound sleep
          And a rest well taken
           To daylight's castle-keep.

In the wildwood
          beyond his panes
The falcons fledged.
            Leaves shed tiles
On the forest floor
          of shadow and light
Until at last
        a darker green
Began to shimmer
          in a sharper wind
And sere leaves
        sailed past the sill
                like pennants of a boat.
          Ripples broke the glass
           Of blue that used to float
         And reflect on clouds that pass
           Over the tower's moat.

Colors flowed
                    over the sill
Out of the woodland,
                              through his panes
Upon the gusts
                    of October wind
Sweeping the leaves
                              from cold tiles
Into piles
                    not of green,
But rainbow strains
                              in a brown light
                                        that fell sifting
                    Out of a lowering sky.
                              The clouds, darkly drifting
                    Where they used to fly
                              Fleetly, did little lifting.

Dawns were darker;
                              there was less light
As the days lengthened.
                              The windowsill
Swallowed shadows.
                              Enkidu sensed
The weather's change,
                              approaching pains.
He must fall
                    upon the tiles
That Enten, god of winter
                              scoured with wind.
                                        The blazing altar
                    Of Enten would not dwindle
                    Nor the solstice falter
                    Till it could not kindle.
                              Then the White God's psalter

Would avail no longer.
                              His prayers would wind
Toward the pole
                    where northern light
Would glance from glaciers
                              laid like tiles
Upon the tundra.
                    Enkidu's sill

Would melt in the glow
　　　　　　of moonlit panes
As April gained
　　　　　　a patina of green,
　　　　　　　　　began to paint
　　　　The meadows with hues of spring
　　　　　　And woods without restraint.
　　　　The mating birds would sing
　　　　　　Above the dove's complaint,

The wind would sough
　　　　　　over the sill,
Warmth would lighten
　　　　　　the night's panes;
Spring would walk
　　　　　on tiles of green
　　　　　　　　　once more.
　　　　Enten would stay asleep
　　　　　　Despite the freshet's roar
　　　　Until the drifts were deep
　　　　　　Around Enkidu's door.

CANTO IV: THE RETURN OF ENKIDU

When at last
            Enkidu returned
To the city of Erech
                Gilgamesh
Was filled with joy.
                He did not know
What had become
                of his soul-brother
Although he had caused
                    the realm to be searched
Far afield
            and near at home.
He could not ask
                Lilitu, for she
Too had vanished.
                "O my friend,"
Said Gilgamesh,
                "I am determined
To go to your
            cedar forest
Where you were born
                    where I will fight
Fierce Humbaba,
                the evil ogre.
I will kill him
                and cut down
His trees
            so that never
Again will he rise
                to raze my kingdom."

Enkidu, astonished,
                replied to his lord,
"Know this, my friend,
                    when I lived there.
I sometimes explored
                    a great distance
From the outskirts
                of the woodland
Deep into its center.
                    There I encountered

The sleepless Humbaba
                        whose roar was a whirlwind,
Whose breath an inferno.
                        Why do you wish
To beset such a monster?
                        Enlil has appointed
Him the sentinel
                        of the Forest of Cedars.
If he hears a mere
                        tread on the trail
He will cry aloud,
                        'Who comes?'
And Humbaba will seize
                        the poacher in his claws.'"

Gilgamesh spoke
                        to his friend and henchman,
"I require the rich
                        yield of the mountains.
I go to the Forest
                        of Cedars to fell
The trees of Humbaba
                        with a mighty axe
Forged by the blacksmiths
                        of my armory.
Who is not
                defeated by Death?
Gods and goddesses,
                        certainly, but mortals
All must fall
                and become wind
Whining among
                        the limbs and boles.
Your own breath
                        says that you fear
The onslaught of battle.
                        If I should fail,
My name shall forever
                        be sung in ballads
That tell it was I
                        who fought with Humbaba.
When you cry me 'Caution!'
                        you grieve my heart,
For I am determined
                        to fell the forest

And to fight Humbaba
                 that I may gain
Fame everlasting.
             The axes are ready,
As are the weapons
              my craftsmen have cast
And made sharp
           for battle. The celts
Of the axes weigh
           three talents
Each. The glaives
          too are monstrous;
Each hilt weighs
        two talents —
The blades, thirty
        manas apiece;
The golden swordblades
           thirty manas."

Then Gilgamesh
          called in his Elders
To counsel with him
           at the Seven-Bolt
Portal of Erech.
         Hearing the rumor,
The citizens and artisans
           gathered in the streets.
Gilgamesh
       addressed the gathering:
"My Eldermen, hear me!
          I go against
Humbaba the Fierce
        who, when he hears,
Shall say, 'let me see
        this Gilgamesh,
Whose fame fills
      many countries.'"

The Elders replied,
        "O Gilgamesh,
You are young,
       you are filled
With the valor of youth.
          You do not know

Fully the danger
          of the monster Humbaba.
Enkidu has gone
          into the forest
And witnessed Humbaba
          in his element.
Listen to his words
          to exercise caution."

But Gilgamesh knelt
          before Shamash,
God of the Sun,
          lifted his hands
And entreated him,
          "I beg that my life
Be spared to return to
          the ramparts of Erech.
I place myself
          under thy aegis."
Shamash replied,
          "Then take with you
Your companion
          the Hero Enkidu,
This I command.
          You must obey
If you wish to return."
          Enkidu bowed
Before the altar
          of the god Shamash.
He agreed to go
          with the expedition
To the Cedar Forest
          which he knew and feared.

The Elders said
          to Gilgamesh,
"Farewell, our Master.
          We have no foreboding
If you will let
          Enkidu lead you,
For he knows the way,
          and he knows the forest —
With his own eyes
          he has seen Humbaba.

Let Enkidu
          be in the van
And you will be safe
              Shamash has sworn.
Wash thy feet
          in a hollow pool
When you make camp,
              and fill thy goatskins
With pure water;
          pour it in homage
To the Sun-god,
          thus to remind
Lugalbanda,
          her devotees,
Hetaera and harlots,
          of your compact
with great Shamash,
          god of the Sun."

Gilgamesh spoke
          to Enkidu, saying,
"Are you fully
          sworn to this foray?
Be not afraid
          for you may trust me."
And forth they marched
             together, the heroes
And their warrior army
          to find the spot
Where Humbaba dwelt
          in the Cedar Forest
              where Enkidu had been born
            among the beasts and meadows
             far from the shepherd's horn
          in sunlight and in shadows,
             where his wolf-hair had been shorn.

CANTO V: THE FOREST OF HUMBABA

Gilgamesh
   and Enkidu strode
Forth from the grand
     gate of the city,
Enkidu leading
    the way from Erech
Toward the forest
    of fearsome Humbaba.
They marched many
    leagues until
At last they approached
     the verge of the woodland
Where Entu the treeherd
    stood sentinel
At the sylvan
    entranceway.
Enkidu lifted
   his eyes and spoke
Unto the monster
    that seemed
Himself a cedar:
    "O Guard of the Forest,
For forty leagues
    I have admired
This timberland
   until I sighted
The towering cedar.
    The wood has no peer.
Six gar your height,
    two gar your breadth.
Your branches pivot
    and interlock —
They were fashioned
    in the city of Nippur!
If I had known
   that such was your grandeur
I might have sensed
    trouble no matter
Wherever I went!"
    Enkidu felt
Fear at the thought
    of the forthcoming fight.

He lay for a day
               and then another,
Prone on his pallet.
                    He did not rise
Till twelve
           days had passed,
And then he called
             Gilgamesh,
"Comrade, you hate me
                    because in Erech
I was afraid
            of the coming combat,
Because I said, 'Friend,
                let us not go
Down to the depths
              of the Forest of Cedars!
My arms are weak,
              hands stricken
With palsy.' You said,
             'Enkidu,
Shall we be cowards?
              You shall surpass
All those who battle.
              You are cunning
And shrewd in the fray.
               Be brave and resist
Both trembling and weakness.
                  Have no fear
Of Death, nor terror
             of what may come.
You have led the way
              here from Erech
And have not flinched
              in duty or friendship.
You have guarded me
              and I will guard you.'
Then let it be so!"
              Enkidu arose
And the heroes stood
              staring abroad
At the height of the cedars,
                  scanned the avenue
Past Entu
           into the wood where

Humbaba dwelt.
>>There was a path
Straight as a spear.
>>>>Its passage was clear.
They could see in the distance
>>>>the Mount of the Cedar,
Home of Immortals,
>>>>the shrine of Irnini,
The cedars' pride,
>>>>raised on the mountain.
The shade was fair,
>>>>full of delight.
Bushes spread there
>>>>with the incense of cedar.

Enkidu said,
>>"While I lay ill
I had a dream
>>>>in which I saw
The two of us
>>>>standing together
High on a peak
>>>>and the peak crumbled
Beneath our feet.
>>>>We were left standing
Alone in a desert.
>>>>The mountain is
Evil Humbaba.
>>>>We'll confront him
And throw down his carcass,
>>>>>>leaving his corpse
Abased at our feet
>>>>upon the morrow."

The morrow dawned
>>>>and they broke their fast,
Eating a morsel,
>>>>then hollowed a pit
In the warm sunlight.
>>>>Enkidu stood
Above it and poured
>>>>a meal for the Mountain.
Then a chill wind blew,
>>>>the breath of Humbaba;

It passed over
            Enkidu and caused
Him to cower and sway
                like corn in a field.
Gilgamesh
         bent to support
Enkidu's hips.
            The firmament roared,
Poured out lightning.
               Earth resounded,
Quaking beneath them.
              Smoke rose
Out of the mountain
            dimming the day.
Flames flew
           from the throat of the cone
And molten stone
            flowed down its sides
As it gorged itself
            till the fires faded
And the hot brands
            turned to ash
                as they fell glowing,
          hastened by the breeze
            like seeds of lightning flowing
          into the forest of trees
            where fires began growing.

Gilgamesh took
         his great axe
And stepped forward,
            the first to set
Foot upon
        the forest path,
And as he began
           to pass Entu,
The treeherd reached
            down with his limbs
From above,
         grasped The King,
And raised him into
           a tangle of branches,
Holding him tightly.
           The sudden attack

Took The King
                    unawares.
Gilgamesh gasped
                    and dropped his axe
From a great height.
                    It fell at the feet
Of Enkidu the Hero
                    who, unthinking,
Picked it up
                    and swung it mightily
Against the trunk
                    of the cedar monster.
The sharp blade
                    sliced through

The massive bole
                    and Entu dropped
Gilgamesh
                    before itself
Fell to the earth.
                    The King also
Plummeted, howling
                    with pain, upon
The forest floor,
                    his bones broken.

Enkidu lifted
                    his arms aloft
To Shamash,
                    God of the Sun,
And cried aloud,
                    "Lo, on that day
In Erech the City
                    before we left,
I heard you swear
                    an oath to The King
That you would aid
                    this great assault
On the Forest of Cedars."
                    Shamash hearkened
And raised mighty
                    winds against
The ogre Humbaba,
                    a wind from the North,

A wind from the South —
                yea, a tempest,
A wind of Evil,
           from East and West —
Eight winds in all:
             a chill wind,
A hot wind,
         a whirlwind spinning
Which seized Humbaba
             before and behind,
That he might go
           neither forward nor backward.

Humbaba surrendered,
            whereupon
He spoke to The King
           but not Enkidu,
"O Gilgamesh,
          I pray you stay
Your hand and be
          my master now,
And I will be
        your own vassal.
Disregard my threats
          against you,
For I will lay down
          all weapons before you."

Enkidu said
         to his twin and comrade,
"Pay no attention
          to these lying oaths
Humbaba spreads
         before us here.
You dare not accept
          his specious offer.
Humbaba must not
         remain alive."
Before The King
         could reply
Enkidu lifted
         his monstrous axe
And with one blow
          cut off the head

Of the horrid ogre.
        It rolled upon
                the ground, one eye staring
          into the sky, the other
       open and balefully glaring
         into Earth the Mother
       with neither sight nor caring.

CANTO VI: ISHTAR'S PROPOSAL

Enkidu looked
        to help his friend
Gilgamesh
       who had fallen
From the limbs of Entu
          and injured himself.
When the doctors had done
          their duties to aid
The King, Enkidu
       washed the blood
From his own body,
       braided the locks
of his hair to descend
        over his shoulders.
He laid aside
     his tattered garments
To don clean ones.
       He put on armlets,
Girded his body
     with a baldric.

The goddess Ishtar
       had been watching
The battle between
      foul Humbaba
And the Heroes
     of great Erech.
Now she spoke
      to the handsome Enkidu:
"Come, my warrior,
      be my bridegroom.
Grant me largesse,
      the fruit of your body.
You shall be
     my wedded husband;
I shall be
    your beloved consort.
I shall furnish
     a fine chariot
For you to ride
     azure and golden,

Pure gold its wheels,
                    its yoke bedecked
With precious stones,
                    each day to be harnessed
To great steeds!
                    Enter our palace
With the fragrance of cedar.
                    When you come in,
Threshold and dais
                    shall meet your tread.
Kings and princes
                    shall do you homage
And bring you yield
                    of mountain and plain
As the tribute due you.
                    The ewes of your flocks
Shall all bear twins,
                    each attaining
The size of a mule.
                    All thy mounts
Shall win fame
                    for their speed."

"Aye," Enkidu
                    replied to the goddess,
"But should I take
                    you in marriage,
What besides
                    my body must
I give you?
                    Oil for your body
And expensive apparel?
                    Bread and victuals —
Divine sustenance
                    for your divinity?
Nectar fit
                    for heaven's royalty
To imbibe?
                    Shall I not be bound
To furnish such things
                    if I marry you?
What would be
                    my advantage?
You are a ruin
                    that gives no shelter

From the weather
                     to any man.
You are merely
                 a rear door
Without resistance
                    to blast or storm.
You are a palace
                  that dashes the heroes
Living in it
                into shards and pieces,
A pitfall covered
                  with twigs and leaves
That will fail and trap
                    him who walks
Upon its surface.
                    You are a bottle
That leaks in the desert,
                      limestone that rots
And lets ramparts
                  crumble in ruins.
You are chalcedony
                  that does not guard;
A sandal that tears
                    and causes its wearer
To fall by the wayside.
                       How many husbands
Have you loved faithfully,
                    who has been your lord
And had the advantage?
                   Let me unfold
The endless roster
                 of your husbands,
And you will vouch
                   the truth of the list:

"Tammuz, your handmaid's
                      consort whom you
Yearly made
                the cause of wailing.
Next, the bird Roller,
                  the gay-feathered,
Whom you swore you loved,
                     yet you smote him,
Breaking his wing —
                  in the grove he stands

Crying, 'My wing!'
     You also loved
A Lion in all
    the strength of his vigor,
But what did you do?
      You dug for him
Seven and seven
     pits to entrap him.
And you loved a Stallion,
       magnificent
In the heat of battle,
      but you betrayed
Him with a spur,
     a bridle and quirt,
Thus forcing him
    to gallop seventeen
Leagues until
    he was exhausted.
You caused his dam's
     lamentation.
You also loved
    a neatherd, a Shepherd —
Daily you
   required that he
sacrifice yeanlings,
      heap charcoal upon you;
Natheless, you smote him,
      transformed him
Into a jackal.
    His own herd boy
Drove him away,
    his own mongrels
Tore his buttocks.
    Oh, and yes,
You loved Ishullanu,
     your sire's gardener:
He brought bouquets
    ceaselessly
And garnished your platters
     with herbs and spices.
You merely cast
   your eyes upon him
And he was smitten.
    'O Ishullanu,'

You said, 'Let me taste
                    of your body's vigor.'
But the gardener said,
                    'What do you ask me?
I have eaten
            only that which
My mother has baked
                    nothing else.
What you would feed me
                    is bread of Transgression,
Milk of Iniquity.'

                    "You heard what he said —
you struck him down,
                    transforming him
Into an insect,
            a crawling spider,
Made him dangle
                    halfway up a house
Where he might not
                    move upward or downward
Lest he be crushed
                    or drowned by drainage.
I have no doubt
            that you would do
To me as you
            have done to all
Your erstwhile lovers,
                    so thank you, but no,
Lady Ishtar,
            I will not be yours
To so mishandle
            and to debase."

When Ishtar heard
            Enkidu's reply
She burst into rage
            and swore revenge.
She hastened to Heaven
                    to her father Anu
And to her mother,
                    the goddess Antu
To whom she said,
            "Beloved parents,

Enkidu has laden
              me with insult!
He tallies my sins,
              declares my iniquities."

Anu replied
              to his sacred offspring,
"Nay, you requested
              that he be your husband,
Your legal lover.
              He gave you answer."

Ishtar knelt
              before her father.
"O Father, make me
              a Heavenly Bull
That may vanquish
              the Hero Enkidu,
And fill his body
              with hellish flame!"

Anu spoke,
              said to the Lady,
"If I should do
              as you ask me to do,
Seven years of leer husks
              shall follow the onslaught.
Will you then gather
              corn for Mankind
And increase fodder
              to feed his cattle?"

"Indeed I shall,"
              Ishtar agreed,
"For I have hoarded
              corn for the cattle."

"Then be it so.
              When the Heroes
And their army
              return to Erech

The Bull of heaven
              will be created

And ready to battle
              to restore your honor."
Thus Anu
          dismissed his daughter
                    who settled in to wait
                for the Bull to be created
          when Enkidu would meet his fate.
            Her anger was unabated —
         he might have been her mate!

CANTO VII: THE BULL OF HEAVEN

When the Heroes returned
                  to Erech, they washed
Their hands in the great
                  river Euphrates.
Then they marched
                upon the highway
Into the city
            Where the folk
Crowded out
           of the great gate
To meet them. Enkidu
              helped to carry
The litter on which
             the injured King
Lay in state.
           He and Gilgamesh
Were greeted and feted,
              feasted and praised.
Then Gilgamesh
         uttered a riddle
Unto the nobles
           of mighty Erech:
"Who is the most
           splendid of heroes?
Who was the most
           famous of giants?"
The nobles replied
           to their warrior king,
"Enkidu is most
           splendid of heroes!
Humbaba was most
           famous of giants!"
Then in his palace
           Gilgamesh
Held high revel.
           When at last
All grew quiet
          and the heroes slept
On their nightly couches
              Enkidu, too,

Fell deeply asleep
                    as in a trance.

At midnight suddenly
                    he heard a noise
And awoke to see
                    what it was.
In the center of the room
                    he saw, glowing
in the flickering light
                    an eerie vision:
His lost love
                    Lilitu standing,
An owl on her shoulder,
                    a wolf beside her.
Enkidu started,
                    jumped from his pallet
Took up his sword.
                    Lilitu spoke.
"Put down your weapon,
                    beloved Enkidu,
I mean you no harm.
                    I thought you should meet
Someone who loves you
                    now that Ishtar
Threatens your life
                    and your companion
Gilgamesh is injured
                    and cannot aid you.
Behold, your son!"
                    She pointed down
At the wolf standing
                    there beside her
Staring upward
                    at Enkidu.
"My son!" he cried.
                    Lilitu nodded.
"Yes, your son,
                    for from your seed
I bore and raised him
                    while you were away.
And this," she said
                    pointing to the owl
That sat on her shoulder,
                    "Is my own daughter,

Though she is no
                    bird of your loins."
The owl, like the wolf,
                              stared at Enkidu,
Lifted her wings
                    and began to fly.
The wolf howled
                    and Enkidu saw
That Lilitu stood
                    before him no longer,
But that two owls
                    flew out of the room
And into the darkness
                         of the starless night.
                                   He followed out the door
                         as the evil birds took flight,
                              the owlet and his whore,
                         till they were out of sight
                              and could be seen no more.

The wolf began
                    to howl again —
Enkidu looked
                    and saw the Bull
Of heaven had entered
                         the palace grounds.

Enkidu roared,
                    his son howled,
Alarm was raised
                         and a hundred men
Descended suddenly
                         upon the Bull
Who stood snorting,
                         breathing flame
Into the melee,
                    casting shadows
That danced and flickered
                              against the walls.
The men were lost,
                    screaming in agony
As they burned.
                    Then two hundred
More arrived —
                    again they burned

As did another
        three hundred warriors.
Then the wolf,
        Enkidu's son,
Dived snarling
        into the fray.
The bull gored
        the great gray beast
And tossed him into
        the roiling shades.
Then Enkidu
        girded his loins
And, straightway leaping
        forward, seized
The Sacred Bull
        by his heavy horns,
Cast him down
        his full length.
He stepped forward
        once again
Took it by
        the thick of its tail,
And smashed it against
        the palace wall
Beating its skull
        till its brains fell out
Upon the cobbles
        of the court.
Enkidu stood
        among the carnage
Until the remaining
        warriors saw
That the Bull was dead.
        They cut him open
And removed its heart
        just as the dawn
Began to break.
        Enkidu took it
And offered it
        in sacrifice
To Shamash,
        God of the Sun.
        Everyone in the courtyard
        drank as a libation

the blood of the ill-starred
bull — each had earned his ration,
and many had been scarred.

When Ishtar saw
                her Bull was dead
She mounted the ramparts
                        of Erech and cried,
"Woe to Enkidu —
                he who, by killing
The Bull of the Heavens
                        makes me lament."

When Enkidu heard
                Ishtar shrieking,
He reached down
                to the Bull's body,
Tore off
        its penis and testicles
And tossed them down
                        before her feet.
"If I could only
                serve you thus
In similar manner,
                I'd make a girdle
Of his entrails."
                Ishtar assembled
Her devotees,
                hetaerae and harlots,
About the phallus to
                        lead their lamenting —
Lilitu was there
                with her owlish daughter.
Enkidu said,
                "Have all the owlets
You like, Lilitu,
                but no more puppies!"
Enkidu's companion
                        Gilgamesh
Called his artisans
                        and masters of craft
To come and portion
                        among them the horns
Of the dead Bull
                that they might make

Ornaments
            and souvenirs
To celebrate
            this great event,
And to each of them
            he gave as well
Thirty minas
            of bluest azure
To use as their settings.
            The two Companions
Offered up
            six measures of oil
To Lugalbanda,
            the King's father.
                      Then the gods took guidance
              among themselves to ask
                how the heroes should advance
            and which taken to task —
              to be punished, perchance.

CANTO VIII: THE DEATH OF ENKIDU

The angry gods
              gathered together
in the Underworld
              to take counsel
Regarding the death
              of the Bull of Heaven,
But the gate was closed
              against Ishtar
Who, when she
              arrived pounded
Upon it and cried,
              "If you do not open
The gate to let me
              enter, then I will
Break the it down!
              I will wrench the lock,
smash the posts
              and force the door!
I will raise the dead
              to eat the living,
And the dead will outnumber
              those who live!"
The gods acceded
              and opened the portal
For Ishtar to enter.
              Shamash spoke
To those assembled:
              "He who has killed
The Bull and Humbaba
              must die, but those
Who aided him —
              Gilgamesh
And his warriors — shall live."
                        The God of the Air,
Enlil, replied,
              "O Sun God, it was
At your behest
              that Gilgamesh
Was sent to slay
              the ogre Humbaba.
The Bull of Heaven
              was the creation

Of august Anu,
                    it was not yours,
But now only
                    Enkidu must die?"

Shamash said,
                    "So be it, Enlil."
Enlil acceded.
                    "So be it," he said.
So be it," agreed
                    the goddess Ishtar.
And so it was
                    that Enkidu was smitten
With a lethal fever
                    that weakened his strength
But killed slowly.
                    When he heard
The gods' decree,
                    Enkidu cursed
Ishtar and her
                    underling Lilitu:
"O hetaera," he cried,
                    "I send you a bitter
Curse that will last
                    for Eternity.
Let desolation
                    lie upon your back
And your desire
                    never be sated.
Let you nevermore
                    sleep in peace,
The street be your dwelling,
                    the shade of a wall
Be your abode.
                    May your feet be scorched
And your thirst be unslaked;
                    may your need be total,
For you are the cause
                    of this fever I bear.
When I lived with the beasts
                    I had no fever,
I had no lust,
                    I had no enemy.
You are the cause
                    of my life gone awry,

And now, too soon,
        it will be over."

Shamash heard
        the curse of Enkidu
And from the heavens
        he called, "Enkidu,
Why do you curse
        the hetaera Lilitu?
She it was
        who showed you how
To eat good bread
        for proper divinity —
Aye, and also
        she gave you wine,
Both white and red
        to drink like a king.
She put a generous
        mantle around you
And gave you your partner
        Gilgamesh
Who gave you a handsome
        divan where
You take your rest;
        also a throne
At his left hand
        where princes come
To do you homage.
        When you die
He will cause the folk
        of Erech to weep;
Damsels and heroes
        to bend to your service
And lament your loss.
        He himself
Will bear the stains
        of blood and weeping.
Your lord will wear
        the skin of a lion
Into the desert
        in lamentation."

Enkidu heard
        the words of Shamash —

They appeased his wrath.
                            He retracted
His curse and blessed
                         the whore Lilitu.
"May princes and monarchs
                            seek you out
And be smitten to commit
                         love upon you,
Smite their breeches
                         in disgust against you.
Let the hero
                  comb out his locks
Who would embrace you.
                         Let his golden
And azure girdle
                  loosen and fall
About his feet.
                Let him entreat
The gods to allow him
                     to enter your body.
May you be left
                as the sacred mother
Of seven owlets,
                all of them brides
Of seven werewolves
                who give you sons."
When he had done,
                exhausted, Enkidu
Fell asleep,
            fell into dream.
Supine, he felt
            Lilitu lie
Prone upon him.
              With both her mouths
She drank the juices
              of his withered body —
                                At last Enkidu died.
              Gilgamesh shed many tears,
                then, setting sorrow aside,
              he gave in to the fears
                of what this death implied.

EPILOGUE

In the desert
            as he wandered
Gilgamesh
            asked himself,
"Shall I not
            die as did
My brother, my twin,
                 the Hero Enkidu?
Is there not
            somewhere on Earth
A plant that grants
            eternal youth?
I shall seek the oracle
            Utnapishtim,
The Seer who survived
              the Flood of Noah."
Reluctantly,
            when he was found
Utnapishtim told
            Gilgamesh
Where to find
            the plant he sought.
But the Seer was given
            eternal youth
Uniquely. He challenged
            the King of Erech
To stay awake
            for seven days
And seven nights.
            Gilgamesh
Fell asleep
            almost at once.
"Hearken, Wife,"
            said the Seer,
"Bake one loaf
            of bread each day
The King is asleep.
            We will place
Them by his bed.
            When he wakens
He will see
            he cannot even

Conquer sleep,"
                    and it was so.
When the King
                    woke and arose,
Dressed to continue
                    his wanderings,
Utnapshtim's wife
                    asked her husband
To offer the king
                    a parting gift:
The place to find
                    a kind of kelp
That could make
                    him young again.

Gilgamesh
                    walked to the ocean
To the spot where
                    the seaweed grew.
He bound to each foot
                    a heavy stone
That he might stride
                    the ocean's floor.
He found the kelp
                    and decided to try
Its powers upon
                    an elderly man
When he arrived
                    back in Erech.
But as he slept
                    one night of the trek,
A serpent slithered
                    into his tent
And stole the plant,
                    shedding its skin
As it departed —
                    Gilgamesh
Saw that the snake
                    had been reborn.
He'd failed in his search,
                    so he returned
To Erech.
                    When he saw its walls
He also saw
                    that they were his

Immortality,
        for they would last
Eternally.
       Alone in his chamber,
He found an utukku
          waiting there:
              the restless spirit of his friend.
        "Tell me the law of Death, Enkidu,
         "Tell me, now you know the end."
        "Alas! I am not allowed to tell you,
          until you join me when you descend."

SELAH.

The oldest long narrative poem in the world, *The Epic of Gilgamesh*, was written in what we would today call "prose prosody," that is to say, in parallel sentence structures such as those to be found in the Torah — the Old Testament, the primary ones being: synonymous parallelism, synthetic parallelism, antithetical parallelism, and climactic parallelism. Prose poems written in parallel structures set up *prose rhythms* that have some of the effect of verse, but they will not be verse because verse is metered language and prose is not. These parallel sentence structures will create rhythms, but they will not create *meters* that are *identical* rhythmic structures.

Constructional schemes, like all *schemes* are strategies for constructing *sentences*. They have to do with *syntax*, the ways in which words, phrases, clauses, and larger units are grammatically balanced in sentences. *Synonymia* or synonymous parallelism, is a *paraphrase* in parallel sentence structures ("I love you; you are my beloved"); *synthesis* or synthetic parallelism, is *consequence* in parallel structures ("I love you; therefore, I am yours"); *antithesis* or antithetical parallelism is the *opposition* of ideas (*antinomy*) expressed in parallel structures ("I love you, and I loathe you"); *auxesis* or climactic parallelism is the building up, in parallel structures, of a *catalog* or *series* that ultimately closes at the *zenith* (high point) of the set, the *climax* ("I love your eyes, hair, breasts; I love the way you walk and speak; I love you"). *Epithonema* is *climactic summation* at the conclusion of a sequence. *Meiosis* is the building up, in parallel structures, of a *catalog* or *series* that ultimately closes at the *nadir* (low point) of the set, the *anticlimax*. ("We struggled through dense forests; we forded raging torrents; we battled the terrors of storm and starvation to reach the road; we took the bus home.")

A "classical" language is one that arose in one of the ancient civilizations such as Hittite, Babylonian, Akkadian, Sumerian, Egyptian (versions of *Gilgamesh* appear in several of these ancient languages), Sanscrit, Greek, and Latin. A "vernacular" language is one that is still in current use that was derived from a classical language; for instance, many of the modern European languages were derived from Latin which is now obsolete except in the Roman Catholic liturgy. Italian, Spanish, Portugese, French, and Rumanian all were derived from the Latin language. The oldest epic written in a European vernacular language is *Beowulf* that was written in the Indo-European language called Old English in a strong-stress verse system or *prosody* called Anglo-Saxon prosody.

Several later English language narrative poems were also written in strong stress verse, such as William Langland's *The Vision of Piers Plowman* and *Sir Gawain and the Green Knight*. Anglo-Saxon prosody has continued to be written fitfully over the centuries, even in contemporary times.

The basis for accentual verse is the counting of *stressed* or *accented* syllables in a line of verse, paying no attention to the number of unstressed syllables. In every word of the English language of two or more syllables, like the stressed syllables in the words **cow**boy and **sing**ing, *at least one syllable will take a stress*. If one cannot at first differentiate the stressed syllable from one that is unstressed, then one may consult a pronouncing dictionary.

Important single-syllable words, particularly *verbs* (like "hear" and "rides") and *nouns* generally take strong stresses. Unimportant single-syllable words in the sentence, such as articles, prepositions, and pronouns (except demonstrative pronouns like "this" and "those") do not take strong stresses, although they may take *secondary* stresses through promotion or demotion, depending on their position in the sentence or the line of verse: in any series of three *unstressed* syllables in a line of verse, one of them, generally the middle syllable, will take a secondary stress through *promotion* and will stand in place of a stressed syllable (for more information on these subjects please see any edition of my *The Book of Forms: A Handbook of Poetics*). In any series of three stressed syllables in a line of verse, one of them, generally the middle syllable, will take a secondary stress through *demotion* and will stand in place of an unstressed syllable. An accent may be forced upon a syllable through *rhetorical stress,* by underlining, italicizing, boldfacing, or otherwise artificially heightening it, as has just now been done (*just, now,* and *been* is a series of unstressed syllables).

The features of Anglo-Saxon prosody are these: each line (called a *stich*) of verse contains four stresses; two or three of these syllables are *over-stressed* by means of *alliteration*. This term means that the first syllable of a word is accented, first, by means of *pronunciation* (that is, the way in which we ordinarily pronounce the word — with the accent on the first syllable, like **cow**boy), and, second, by means of the *repetition* of *consonant sounds* (that is, in two or more words the stressed first syllable begins with a sound of the alphabet other than the *vowels* a, e, i, o, or u.

Besides the four strong stresses in the stich and the alliterations, each stich is broken in half by a pause called a *caesura*. This pause is built into the poem in one way or another (by phrasing, punctuation, or sound, like two s sounds coming together so that the reader or speaker must pause to distinguish them: (the goats / scrambled). In this excerpt from *Beowulf* the champion of the Geats learns of the monster Grendel who terrorizes Denmark, and he sails to help King Hrothgar:

from THE EPIC OF BEOWULF

In Geatland Beowulf,
                    Higlac's hallmate,
Greatest of the Geats,
                    greater and stronger
Than any other

            anywhere else,
Heard that Grendel
                 turned the halls
Of distant Heorot
                 to scenes of horror.
He ordered a ship
                 be readied to sail
Over the ocean,
                 for he would help
Hrothgar the Dane
                 in his hour of need.
The wise elders
                 of the gathered Geats
Did not object,
                 for the portents promised
Success for their hero
                 in far Heorot,
They said farewell
                 as he fared forth
With a chosen band
                 of brave brothers.
Fourteen of the finest
                 that could be found
Among the Geats
                 who boarded their boat
And set sail
                 on the wild waves,
Pointing their prow
                 to distant Denmark
Far from their fjords,
                 their familiar fields,
Coursing the currents
                 beneath the cliffs,
Eager to find
                 what would befall them
And their longboat
                 laden with armor,
Lined with shields
                 along the gunwales,
Their oaken hearts
                 in their oaken vessel
Beating strongly
                 as the wild wind
Hurled them beyond
                 the foaming breakers

Until at last
          they saw in the sea,
Rising out
          of the furling froth,
Hills lifting
          their green heads
On the horizon,
          and soon they stood
Under those cliffs
          where their cruise ended.

I remember very early in my life running across both prose prosody (called "free verse" back then) and Anglo-Saxon prosody, the former in the Bible (I was a preacher's son) and in the work of Walt Whitman; the latter in a children's encyclopedia, *The Book of Knowledge*. Since childhood I have been interested in all things having to do with language, literature, and in particular poetry — I began seriously studying its structure and writing verse by the time I entered high school:

I first read Walt Whitman's poem "Mannahatta" in my 11th-grade English class. Perhaps it would be as well to quote the Whitman poem, just to refresh my own and the reader's memory. I quote from Whitman's *Selected Poems,* edited by Arthur Stedman in 1892, the year of the poet's death:

I was asking for something specific and perfect for my city,
Whereupon lo! upsprang the aboriginal name.

Now I see what there is in a name, a word, liquid, sane, unruly,
      musical, self-sufficient,
I see that the word of my city is that word from of old,
Because I see that word nested in nests of water-bays, superb,
Rich, hemm'd thick all around with sailships and steamships, an
      island sixteen miles long, solid-founded,
Numberless crowded streets, high growths of iron, slender, strong,
      light, splendidly uprising toward clear skies,
Tides swift and ample, well-loved by me, toward sundown,
The flowing sea-currents, the little islands, larger adjoining island,
      the heights, the villas,
The countless masts, the white shore-steamers, the lighters, the ferry-
      boats, the black sea-streamers well-model'd,
The down-town streets, the jobbers' houses of business, the houses of
      business of the ship-merchants and money-brokers, the river-
      streets,
Immigrants arriving, fifteen or twenty thousand in a week,

The carts hauling goods, the manly race of drivers of horses, the
    brown-faced sailors,
The summer air, the bright sun shining, and the sailing clouds aloft,
The winter snows, the sleigh-bells, the broken ice in the river,
    passing along up or down with the flood-tide or ebb-tide,
The mechanics of the city, the masters, well-form'd, beautiful-faced,
    looking you straight in the eyes,
Trottoirs throng'd, vehicles, Broadway, the women, the shops and
    shows,
A million people — manners free and superb — open voices —
    hospitality — the most courageous and friendly young men,
City of hurried and sparkling waters! city of spires and masts!
City nested in bays! My city!

I'd not yet read a great deal of Whitman, and it was shortly after the
class had read "Mannahatta" that I took my first trip to Manhattan and
saw for myself what Whitman's city had become in the twentieth century.
The vague sense of offense I'd felt when I read his poem crystallized, after
the trip, into a lifelong aversion to the work of "The Good Gray Poet." Yet,
in a curious sense, my negative response to Whitman was as formative for
me as a positive response has been for many another writer. He was the
motivating force behind the writing of my first ambitious poem, which
was also my longest poem to that date, the most serious, and the most
consciously formal, in contrast with what I perceived at the time to be the
aformal splatter of Whitman's good gray prose poetry.

I don't recall the occasion of the field trip in my junior year to New
York City, ninety miles away from Meriden, Connecticut, down the Merritt
Parkway, but it was an excursion by bus. Not much remains in my memory
of the outing. I do remember we saw "Chinatown" and the Bowery. I recol-
lect the skyscraper canyons and the dirt. But there is one image that is still
vivid — it was of a derelict on the Bowery. He was, or he seemed to be,
an old man. I saw him up close. He wore a tattered T-shirt and a pair of
the palest blue denim "dungarees" (a.k.a. "blue Jeans") frayed around his
ankles, no shoes, his toenails long and filthy. He wore an old rope for a belt.

The creases of skin on his face were filled with dirt, and in his ears
the dirt was caked like topsoil. His hair was white; it fell down over his
eyes, which were as pale blue as his jeans — washed out, empty, the eyes
of a chronic alcoholic. He was panhandling. It was a dismaying and disil-
lusioning experience, to say the least, to be brought face-to-face with this
wrecked human being amid the squalid alleys of New York. I returned
home considerably troubled by what I had seen of Whitman's "prophetic"
vision of America.

Not long after the trip I began to write some poems about my experi-
ences in and impressions of Manhattan, one in particular:

THE CITY

This is the city,
the grime and the dust;
the rushing, roaring, rampant stream of life
passing,
        pressing,
                pushing along the narrow streets;
the clash and clatter of machines and fuming engines;
the hosts of peering people
leaning from towering tenements,
fouling the air with curses and guttural mutterings;
the acrid stench, the air heavy, dead —
whiskey-tainted and oil-smeared;
anachronisms taunting, fighting, drinking
and collapsing in filth-laden gutters;
rich men getting richer, poor men staying poor;
rich and poor alike: miserable and selfish, greedy and
        hellbound.

This is the city…,
citadel of humanity;
decadent, fruitless;
its glittering veneer a mockery
hiding a core of misery.
This is the palace of Mankind,
the fortress of a futile race,
the pinnacle of Civilization…,

        this…
                is the City!

It was not until my senior year, however, that I conceived of the epic scheme of my adolescence, "Observations of a Resurrected Corpse," as I originally titled my English Honors class project, which was excerpted for publication in the class periodical, *The Leaky Pen*. That year it won some prizes both in the state and nationally, and a dozen years later I still thought well enough of my first earnest attempt to court the Muse to take it out and revise it once more, this time for full publication in a little magazine. In revising it I changed its title to "The City's Mask," and I emphasized its inherently dramatic form:

THE CITY'S MASK

Persons of the masque:
    A Corpse
    Chorus of Townsfolk

Place of the masque: a graveyard near a city at the present time. During the first portion of the masque the city is nearly obscured by a fog. As the action progresses the city becomes more clearly defined, until at last it is illuminated by a garish yellow light. As the masque opens, the Corpse is discovered standing outside the graveyard.

Corpse.   The earth is good.
           I am grateful, satisfied with life.
           Nature's treasure is my heritage,
           and equilibrium of mind is mine —
           worldly things I neither own nor want;
           tranquility and work suffice for me.
           My life is pleasure's bed.

(He moves inside the graveyard, kneels before a stone.)

           But I come to Death.
           Abysms engulf my tired flesh.
           Sleep enfolds me; the darkness here is dense.
           Dreams writhe fitfully upon the verge
           of consciousness, but cannot penetrate
           this stratum of existence. Now and then
           I sense a surge towards life...,

(He rises.)

           I awaken!
           Up, dank bones! and walk among mankind.
           Wind and sun once more caress my flesh.
           Let me pause a time and look about;
           nearby, what? — here stands a morose crowd
           of men and women who deploy like sorrow
           about this granite forest.

At this point the reader might pause and look at the form a high school
poet chose to use for these soliloquies by his protagonist — that form has
not been changed from the original. The first line of each stanza is iam-
bic dimeter, accentual-syllabic verse, and each last line is iambic trimeter;
thus, the first and last lines of each stanza, taken together, equal one line
of iambic pentameter verse which was, in effect, broken at the caesura into
two lines ("line-phrased" or *lineated*). The five lines intervening between
are unrhymed iambic pentameter as well (*blank verse*, not "free verse").
Whenever the Corpse talks to himself, he uses this stanza.

His dialogues with the chorus, however, are in rhymed heroic (iam-
bic pentameter) couplets: this is a change from the original, which used
iambic tetrameter rhyming couplets. Perhaps when I revised the poem for
publication I wanted a little extra space in the line to orate, or tetrameters
felt too short for the gravity of the speeches. The Corpse is still speaking:

> As I stand among these muted graves
> beggar, churchman, chandler, — saints and knaves
> wearing their solitary cloaks of gloom —
> stand in the shadow of my cast-off tomb.
> Their mouths begin to writhe. I hear them sigh:

Chorus.   What was it like to sleep in the soil, to lie
breathless beneath the rock, your mortal breath
stopped by a mute of sand? Tell us of Death —
what song does he strum upon his solemn lute?
Does Peace come piping quietly with his flute,
filling the earth with the harmony of things?
Or do men's frenzied bones dance in the night
to the drums of Fear? Is there second sight,
or only the blind worm tunneling through recall?
Is Death a passage through this mortal wall?
Tell us. We wish to know, for we have seen
all that we care to of this wild careen
of planets and futile works through vacant space.

Incidentally, I might point out here that this is the question *Gilgamesh*
poses to the phantom of his dead friend *The Hero Enkidu*. It is the question
every human being has asked in every period of humanity's existence.

Corpse.   You amaze me, mortals. Of what place
and time are you, of what hopeless race?
Are the men all gone, replaced by mannequins
hollow inside? Or is this Hell were sins
shall be scourged by mockery instead of flame?
Don't ask me to number things I cannot name.

> Rather, if you be made of virile marrow
> go live in the world. Rejoice before you sorrow.

Chorus. We've known the world, and were it not for fear
> of the unknown, we'd trade you our career
> for your contentment, if Death be content.
> This planet's virile youth, and ours, is spent
> with waste and wars; Nature's vicious rape
> has been accomplished by the hairless ape.
>
> Since you cannot impart your history
> of sleep, we'll tell you ours — a wakeful story
> that has to do with people piled on people
> in dens of stone taller than any steeple.
> We'll talk of a place called Megalopolis...

(The chorus points in the direction of the city, which is now clearly defined):

> ...it lies there yonder. Listen, we'll speak of this
> the contagious city.

At this point in the original I broke into what my teachers had been trying to define as "free verse," a concept I struggled to understand then and for many years thereafter — how can you have metrical (that is, counted) verse that is "free." I wanted to answer Whitman directly, in his own idiom. These tirades were the original portions of "Observations of a Resurrected Corpse," written the year before, and everything else had been written to frame them. But when I came to revise the poem, I had learned enough of poetics and the traditions of English poetry to realize that, rather than writing "free verse," I had come very close, altogether unwittingly, to writing in Anglo-Saxon prosody; that is to say, in alliterative accentual verse with a medial caesura or pause in the center of the line, rather than in prose parallels in the manner of Whitman (compare the following passage with the original poem "The City," above). Therefore, in revising I went all the way and deliberately cast the fulminations of the chorus in Anglo-Saxon prosody:

> See it clearly:
> a ghetto of grime,   of grit and mire,
> a roiling, roaring,   raging torrent
> of life passing, pressing,   pushing along
> the narrow alleys,   canyons of brick;
> the clash and clamor   of crowds and engines,
> the pyramids of people   peering and leaning

from towering tenements,   tainting the air
with curses and calls,   the cries of Cain;
the acrid aroma,   the air leaden;
the rich growing richer,   the poor still poor,
rich or poor,   greedy alike
with the avarice of vermin,   vicious, despairing.

(It was this passage in particular that infuriated my English teacher who
declared in class, smashing his fist on the desk, that it contained the seeds
of Communism: these were the Red-eyed 1950s.)

This is the city,   citadel of Man —
decadent, desperate,   dollar-driven,
its veneer of glass   a transparent mockery,
a mural of mirror   masking a core
of misery and madness: humanity's castle,
the fabulous fortress   of a futile race,
the pinnacle of pride,   the prime of civility.
See it clearly.   This is the city.

Corpse.   I have to see.
Let me emerge from the chill crypt's mouth.
I shall judge this world of which the folk
standing near my grave have thus discoursed.
Out upon the wings of the bruiting wind
and swiftly through the countryside I'll go
to find the fabled city.

(*As he speaks, he moves quickly into the city.*)

Where trees once stood   there stands a wall;
where once grass grew,   grim buildings rise;
where forest lanes wandered,   there writhes a highway;
where once was solitude,   a city screams.
Lights, noise impinge   on revolted senses;
soot and dust   and smog and grease
replace silent   leaves and loam.
Neons glaring;   carhorns blaring
cacophonies   of crimson sound!
Where once flowed lucid,   plashing brooks
there now splash streams   of sewage and silt;
where there were scents   of the subtle spices
of summer and winter,   spring and fall,
slums exude   the stench of Death.
The world is an apple,   once plump and ripe,

now smitten   with the bitter blight
of burgeoning burgs — a blitz of cities!

Through the streets
of Megalopolis I walk and wonder.
On every side the city's squalor gasps.
I must gasp myself, for none of this
is part of my green remembrance of the past.
Sense revolts within me as I look
at the squalid town.

The city screams!   see its furor;
hear its raging,   madcap uproar!
Watch the crushing,   nerve-crazed crowds
prowling around   the spires and towers
that stand like sticks   stuck in an anthill
under the unctuous,   oily clouds.
The city stands,   surly and painted,
a festering female   whose foul wares
are hawked and bought   with ostentation.
The sin-slaked lips   and sallow flesh
of this lusting leper   are lent to lechers
who flock like flies   to her flimsy skirts —
the silken skirts   that screen her body.
The city stands   screams her trade.

(*As the Corpse retraces his steps toward the graveyard, the city begins to fade.*)

I'll return
to the graveyard where I should have stayed.
At least, Death is tranquility compared
with this. Time, in your mercy, let me lie

— I am astonished to discover, or I should say to realize, for the first time as I type this memoir, that this last line, which was part of the original draft, is a paraphrase of lines from Dylan Thomas' "Fern Hill." But perhaps it should not be surprising, for these were the years when Thomas was wandering about the United States declaiming his wonderful verse, though I was never to encounter him in the living flesh. I do remember picking up, in 1953 at the Yale Co-Op in New Haven, the new edition of his *Collected Poems* —

once more beneath the sod! Take back these bones
that they may fuse once more with stone. Give me
my niche with the forgotten.

Upon my marker lies my threadbare shroud,

(he picks it up and puts it on);

and nearby there still stands the mortal crowd
which once I envied, now may only pity
since I have made my survey of the city.
What is that sound they make as I approach? —

Chorus.   You've seen why we'd be thankful to encroach
upon your simple slot of hallowed earth.
The lives of men in mass have slender worth.

Corpse.   Oh! Lord of all creation, is this your Man?
Image of the Ideal, whose life began
swaddled in primal Nature's verdant sheets
but ends within the city's sordid streets?
Farewell, mortals, Death shall be my choice.
I shall respond henceforth to no carnal voice,
but lie in clay until all cities sink
into the muck of ages, until the stink
of their hacking funnels exhale the scent of night
and neon fades beneath Aurora's light.

(Once more he kneels before his stone.)

To sleep again —
back to blankness, back to the nether-land.
Sanity's a figment and a fraud;
only madness reigns eternally.
Reliquary, hold my bones until
the morning after history, when Earth
is frost among the stars.

None of this, however, explains my fascination with Anglo-Saxon al-
literative verse. Not many years later I ran across the wonderful epic titled
Gawain and the Green Knight by an anonymous English poet. The Middle
Ages are often called "the Dark Ages," even by people who should know
better. One of the reasons they seem dark, perhaps, is that we know very
little about certain seminal figures of the period. In English literature, for
instance, many people would recognize the name of Geoffrey Chaucer,
even if they have not struggled to read the works he wrote in Middle Eng-
lish, a language form that seems a good deal more foreign to speakers of
modern English than it actually is.

As a teacher of literature I have often wondered if the lack of biographical detail about certain writers has not had more to do than it should with the fact that they are often ignored in the classroom. Do we teach great literature, or are we rather teachers of "historical" literary figures — of periods and trends rather than of poems, plays, and fiction?

We know a good deal about Chaucer, but what do we know of William Langland? How many even recognize the name of the author of the piece commonly known as *Piers Plowman*? When was the last time that someone other than a scholar or graduate student read the work of John Gower or of John Lydgate, both better poets than many currently studied?

There were other writers, some of them contemporaries of Chaucer, whose work may be as important, of whom we know very little. Information about these men and women, such as Marie de France, a Norman English poet, is hard to come by sometimes. This is so partly owing to a paucity of certain records; but it is so also because artists of the Middle Ages did not create in hopes of being known to posterity. Rather, they created for particular contemporary audiences — their leige-lords, perhaps, or the church. And Medieval writers did not write for publication, as we do, because publication as we know it had not yet been invented.

William Dunbar, the Scottish post-Chaucerian poet who thrived *circa* 1460 to 1520, wrote a great poem that one might perhaps call a "chronicle elegy." Its title is "Lament for the Makars [makers, poets]," and in it he wrote at one point,

> Clark of Tranent, too, [Death has] slain,
> Who wrote The Adventures of Gawain;...

Tranent is situated in the Scottish county of East Lothian, approximately a mile from the seacoast of the Firth of Forth. According to George Ellis in his *Specimens of the Early English Poets* (London: Henry Washbourne, 1845), a contemporary of Dunbar, the so-called "rhyming chronicler of Scotland" Andrew "Wyntown, in his account of king Arthur, mentions, among the historians of his Gests, an author who is totally unknown to our poetical antiquaries. He calls him 'Huchown of the Awle Ryale,' and tells us that

> He made the great Gest of Arthur,
> And the adventure of Sir Gawain;
> The 'Pistle [epistle, letter] als[o] of Sweet Susanne.

Mr. Macpherson seems to think that Huchown (Hugh) may be the Christian name of the Clark [clerk] of Tranent,

> That made the adventures of Sir Gawain,

(Dunbar's "Lament," &c);..."

The largest problem with the candidacy of Hugh Clark of Tranent, if that was the name of Dunbar's poet, or with any other putative Scottish author of *Sir Gawain and the Green Knight*, is the fact that the form of English in which he wrote was not Scots but a Middle English dialect located in the Midlands around northwestern Staffordshire and southeastern Cheshire.

An often-suggested candidate for the authorship of the poem is John Massey who hailed from Cotton, Cheshire, believed by some scholars to have penned the poem *St. Erkenwald* that bears stylistic resemblances to *Gawain* and is written in a dialect similar to that of *The Pearl*, but not all scholars agree on the dating of *Saint Erkenwald* and the anonymity of the author(s) of all these poems continues in force.

The *Gawain* Poet has been called "Ricardian" by J. A. Burrow, author of *Ricardian Poetry, Chaucer, Gower, Langland and the Gawain Poet*, because all four writers were more or less contemporary with one-another during the reign of the grandson of Edward III, Richard II of England (January 6, 1367 – c. February 14, 1400), but Geoffrey Chaucer (c. 1343 – 25 October 1400) and John Gower (c. 1330 – October 1408), both court poets, wrote in a London-area dialect, whereas William Langland (c. 1332 – c. 1386) was, like the Gawain poet, a Midlands native. Both Gower and Chaucer, who knew each other personally, wrote poems in the system that would eventually be called "accentual-syllabics" and become the standard prosody of modern English verse, whereas Langland and the Gawain poet continued to practice versions of Anglo-Saxon prosody.

In the Foreword of her great book of Medieval history titled *A Distant Mirror: The Calamitous 14th Century*, Barbara W. Tuchman wrote that Enguerrand de Coucy VII, who lived from 1340-1397, "Through marriage to the eldest daughter of the King of England [...] acquired a double allegiance bridging two countries at war," that is to say, France and England. She wrote further that "...except for a single brief article published in 1939, nothing has been written about him in English, and no formal, reliable biography in French except for a doctoral thesis of 1890 that exists only in manuscript. I like finding my own way" (xiv–xv).

Unfortunately, Ms. Tuchman was wrong, for a wonderful book that touched on her subject had been written by Henry Littleton Savage and published in 1956, thirty-three years earlier, *The Gawain-Poet, Studies in His Personality and Background* (Chapel Hill: University of North Carolina). Savage's treatise is the only book of literary scholarship I have ever run across that reads like a fine work of detective fiction, keeping one in suspense waiting for the ultimate revelation of the authorship of Gawain until the very last sentence which I will not give away any more than I would divulge the ending of a novel by Tony Hillerman.

How Ms. Tuchman missed this book is baffling to me, for her bibliography in *A Distant Mirror* has the appearance of being exhaustive. She comments on many poets, particularly those who were Continental, but she also treats at reasonable length of Geoffrey Chaucer, John Gower, and

William Langland. Nowhere, however, does she discuss the *Gawain* poet, or even mention a single work attributed to that bard who is arguably of equal stature with Chaucer, the so-called "Father of English Poetry." It was Savage's thesis that the author of *Sir Gawain and the Green Knight* was a poet who was attached to the English estates of Enguerrand, Sire de Coucy, focus of Tuchman's book and the spouse of Princess Isabella, eldest daughter and the second child of Edward III of England and his queen, Philippa.

Princess Isabella was senior to the Sire de Coucy by about eight years — an old maid, in fact, for several of her engagements to other French nobles had fallen through in one way or another. She had been jilted on several occasions, and she herself had done the jilting in one situation. Apparently, however, she was quite pleased, perhaps even overjoyed, to marry Coucy at long last. In any case, Tuchman wrote, "Whether to win over Enguerrand, or because he had taken a personal liking to him, Edward had already in 1363 restored him to full possession of the lands in Yorkshire, Lancaster, Westmoreland, and Cumberland inherited from his great-grandmother" (207).

If the *Gawain* poet was a servant of one of the most powerful members of the English and French nobilities, he was a member in good standing of the society of his time, for every Medieval monarch or great nobleman was the patron of at least one bard. Bards were status symbols. As has elsewhere above been noted, both John Gower and Geoffrey Chaucer were poets of the London court. The Gawain poet may have been as well, but perhaps it is more likely that he was the resident bard at one of the Sire de Coucy's estates elsewhere in Britain, though without a doubt he spent time occasionally in London as well. He must have done if his mistress was the favorite daughter of King Edward III.

There have been many editions of the works of the *Gawain* poet, but the one I like best is *The Complete Works of the Gawain Poet,* edited and translated by the late American poet John Gardner, which takes a giant step toward the rehabilitation of one of the greatest of Middle English authors. Because the nineteenth century admired his poem *The Pearl,* he has been known as the *Pearl* Poet; and because the twentieth century admired another of his poems, *Sir Gawain and the Green Knight,* the author is also known as the *Gawain* Poet. But whoever he was, he was a master.

Because the *Gawain* Poet wrote, unlike Chaucer, in a dialect that did not eventually turn into modern English, he or she is more difficult to read in the original. Again, unlike Chauucer, the *Gawain* poet wrote in the ancient (and often beautiful) alliterative tradition of Old English narrative poetry. This tradition, admittedly somewhat strange to our ears, gave way to the pattern, set by Chaucer and Gower, of accentual-syllabic verse, a tradition which until recently we considered to be "normal" for poetry, although at the present moment in the twenty-first century the hegemony of "free verse" — that is, lineated prose poems — threatens to obliterate not only such poems as *Gawain* but also the entire history of metrical verse, at least in America. Partly for these reasons, the several masterpieces of the *Gawain* Poet have languished.

In his book John Gardner gathered all the known and attributed work of the poet including — besides "Gawain" and "The Pearl" — "Purity," "Patience," and "St. Erkenwald." He presented the pieces in brilliant contemporary translations and discussed the work of the poet and the period in a lucid and helpful introduction.

Anglo-Saxon prosody has continued to be written fitfully over the centuries, even in contemporary times by such people as Richard Wilbur, and there are other, more modern strong stress forms, such as Gerard Manley Hopkins' variable accentual "sprung rhythm" system and William Carlos Williams' triversen stanza.

The English "bob and wheel" is an accentual-syllabic quintet appended as a tail or coda to a stanza of Anglo-Saxon prosody in one Medieval romance in particular, *Sir Gawain and the Green Knight*. The "bob" is a one-or-two-foot line running on (enjambed) from the alliterative accentual stanza, and it is continued by the "wheel," a quatrain of short lines, generally of three feet, rhyming *baba*. The whole quintet "bob and wheel" rhymes *ababa*, but rhyme does not necessarily appear anywhere in the part of the stanza that is made of Anglo-Saxon prosody. The bob rhymes with lines two and four of the wheel; lines one and three of the wheel rhyme with each other. *Gawain* is thus a clear example of the old alliterative verse system being deliberately linked to the new accentual-syllabic prosody invented by Chaucer and Gower. It is thus about as clear a transformational poem as anyone might hope to see coming out of the Middle Ages and linking with modernity.

Sir Gawain and the Green Knight is too long to quote here in its entirety, of course, but this is stanza 25 from the poem in my own modern version (the line, "...and of delight" is the "bob"; the rest of that stanza is the "wheel"):

from SIR GAWAIN AND THE GREEN KNIGHT

> From the deeps of dream
>   Gawain mumbled,
> Suffering stounds [moments]
>   of sorrow and worry
> That Weird [fate] that day
>   would wield him death
> At the Chapel Green
>   where the green man
> Would deal him death
>   with a great dunt [knock, blow].
> Anon our knight
>   recalled his wits,
> Fought his way

                    from the fens [marshes] of slumber,
Rose fleetly
                to attend his fate.
The sweet carline [young woman]
                                    came laughing,
Kissed his face
                and fondled him;
Gawain gladly
                welcomed her kindness,
Admired her garb,
                        her glorious hair,
Faultless features
                    and radiant hue.
Gladness arose
                out of his heart.
He took her there
                in rapture rare,
In ecstasies
                of blissful song
                            and of delight.
        They shared this happy state
        In loving talk and light!
        What might have been his fate
        Had Mary not kept her knight?

                    — The Gawain Poet

I will end this discussion with a note about how *The Hero Enkidu* came to be written. For several years recently I was involved with the publication of two anthologies of sestinas, *The Incredible Sestina Anthology* edited by Daniel Nester (Austin, TX: Write Bloody Press, 2013) and *Obsession: Sestinas in the Twenty-First Century,* edited by Carolyn Beard Whitlow and Marilyn Krysl (Hanover: NH: Dartmouth College Press, 2014). This is the description and definition of the poem form called "sestina" as it appears in my *The Book of Forms: A Handbook of Poetics,* Fourth Edition, (Hanover, NH: The University Press of New England, 2012):

The **SESTINA** is of Medieval French origin, attributed to Arnaut Daniel in the late 12th century and used by other Gallic poets and by Italians including Petrarch and Dante (from whom it received its Italian name). The popularity of the poem in English is primarily a 20th century phenomenon, however, particularly in the United States. The six *end-words* or *teleutons* of the lines of the first stanza are repeated *in a specific order* as end-words in the five succeeding sestet stanzas. In English the sestina is generally written in iambic pentameter or, sometimes, in decasyllabic meters. Its thirty-nine lines are divided into six sestet stanzas and a final triplet envoy (or *envoi*), *q.v.* In the envoy the six teleutons are also picked up, one of them being buried in, and one finishing each line.

The order in which the end-words are repeated appears to have its roots in numerology, but what the significance of the pattern was originally is now unknown. The sequence of numbers is 6-1-5-2-4-3. Obviously, the series is just 1-2-3-4-5-6 with the last three numbers reversed and inserted ahead of the first three: 6-1-5-2-4-3. If the end-words of stanza one are designated ABCDEF (the capital letters signifying repetitions) and the sequence 615243 is applied to it, the order of repetitions in the second stanza will be FAEBDC. Apply the sequence to the second stanza, and the third stanza will be CFDABE. Continuing the process will give us ECBFAD in the fourth stanza, DEACFB in the fifth, and BDFECA in the sixth sestet. The order of repetition in the three lines of the envoy is BE / DC / FA.

While I was involved with this form over the years, I had written a number of experimental sestinas, one of which, "The Obsession," about my father's death and its effect on me, had a lot to do with my involvement with the Dartmouth volume, *Obsession: Sestinas in the Twenty-First Century.* During the summer of 2013 I decided that I wanted to write a sestina such as no one had ever attempted before, to wit, in Anglo-Saxon prosody with bobs and wheels, in the manner of *Gawain and the Green Knight,* and this was the result:

THE GREEN KNIGHT AND THE WHITE

In mad March   the knight in green
Began to waken.   The wild wind
Roared at the door,   rattled the panes —
He lifted his lids   to squint at light
Falling across   the frosty sill
Onto the floor   where chill tiles
                challenged him
        To step into the day
            Where sunshine and the grim
        Mists of morning lay
           In shades both bright and dim.

As time flew   it turned the tiles
From bone white   to warm green.
Flowers bloomed   under the sill,
Soothed by the sun,   stroked by the wind

That wandered whispering   in the June light
That daily rose   and fell through the panes.
                              Out of the deep
                Darkness the knight would awaken
                    From his sound sleep
                And a rest well taken
                    To daylight's castle-keep.

In the wildwood   beyond his panes
The falcons fledged.   Leaves shed tiles
On the forest floor   of shadow and light
Until at last   a darker green
Began to shimmer   in a sharper wind
And colored leaves   fell past the sill
                              like pennants of a boat.
                Ripples broke the glass
                    Of blue that used to float
                And reflect on clouds that pass
                    Over the castle's moat.

Colors flowed   over the sill
Out of the woodland,   through his panes
Upon the gusts   of October wind
Sweeping the leaves   from cold tiles
Into piles   not of green,
But rainbow strains   in a brown light
                              that fell sifting
                Out of a lowering sky.
                    The clouds, darkly drifting
                Where they used to fly
                    Fleetly, do little lifting.

Dawns are darker;   there is less light
As the days lengthen.   The windowsill
Swallows shadows.   The good Green
Knight senses   approaching pains.
He must fall   upon the tiles
That the Knight of winter   will scour with the wind.
                                        The blazing altar
                Of Yuletide will not dwindle
                    Nor the solstice falter
                Until it cannot longer.
                    Then the White Knight' psalter

Will avail no longer.   His prayers will wind

Toward the pole   where northern light
Will glance from glaciers   laid like tiles
Upon the tundra.   The Green Knight's sill
Will melt in the glow   of moonlit panes
As April gains   a patina of green,
                                        begins to paint
                          The meadows with hues of spring
                                  And woods without restraint.
                          The mating birds will sing
                                  Above the dove's complaint,

The wind will sough   over the sill,
Warmth will lighten   the night's panes;
Spring will walk   on tiles of green
                                    once more.
                          The White Knight will stay asleep
                                  Despite the freshet's roar
                          Until the snow is deep
                                  Around the Green Knight's door.

Not long afterward I began work on *Enkidu,* and of course I had to incorporate this poem into it, as I mentioned in the acknowledgments at the beginning of the book.

ABOUT THE AUTHOR

Lewis Turco, Professor Emeritus of English, founder of the Creative Writing program at SUNY Oswego and of the Cleveland Poetry Center, is the author of over fifty chapbooks, monographs, and volumes including *The Book of Forms: A Handbook of Poetics*, known as "the poet's Bible" through four editions since its publication in 1968; *Visions and Revisions of American Poetry*, winner of the Melville Cane Award for Criticism of the Poetry Society of America in 1986; and of *A Book of Fears*, winner of the first annual Bordighera Bilingual Poetry Prize in 1998. Professor Turco was also recipient in 1999 of the second annual John Ciardi Award for Lifetime Achievement in Poetry given by the National Italian American Foundation. He holds a BA from the University of Connecticut, an MA from the University of Iowa, and honorary doctorates from Ashland University, the University of Maine at Fort Kent, and Unity College in Maine.

VIA FOLIOS
A refereed book series dedicated to the culture of Italians and Italian Americans.

ALBERT TACCONELLI, *Perhaps Fly,* Vol. 106, Poetry, $14

RACHEL GUIDO DEVRIES, *A Woman Unknown in Her Bones,* Vol. 105, Poetry, $11

BERNARD J. BRUNO, *A Tear and a Tear in My Heart,* Vol. 104, Non-Fiction/Memoir, $20

FELIX STEFANILE, *Songs of the Sparrow,* Vol. 103, Poetry, $30

FRANK POLIZZI, *A New Life with Bianca,* Vol. 102, Poetry, $10

GIL FAGIANI, *Stone Walls,* Vol. 101, Poetry, $14

LOUISE DESALVO, *Casting Off,* Vol. 100, Fiction, $22

MARY JO BONA, *I Stop Waiting for You,* Vol. 99, Italian/American Poetry, $12

RACHEL GUIDO DEVRIES, *Stati Zitta, Josie,* Vol. 98, Children's Literature, $8

GRACE CAVALIERI, *The Mandate of Heaven,* Vol 97, Italian American Poetry, $11

MARISA FRASCA, *Via Incanto: Poems from the Darkroom,* Vol. 96, Italian American Poetry, $12

DOUGLAS GLADSTONE, *Carving a Niche for Himself: The Untold Story of Luigi Del Bianco and Mount Rushmore,* Vol. 95, Italian American History, $12

MARIA TERRONE, *Eye to Eye,* Vol. 94, Poetry, $15

CONSTANCE SANCETTA, *Here in Cerchio: Letters to an Italian Immigrant,* Vol. 93, Italian/American Studies, $15

MARIA MAZZIOTTI GILLAN, *Ancestors' Song,* Vol. 92, Poetry, $14

MICHAEL PARENTI, *Waiting for Yesterday: Pages from a Street Kid's Life,* Vol. 90, Memoir, $15

ANNIE RACHELE LANZILLOTTO, *Schistsong,* Vol. 89, Poetry/Gay Studies/Women Authors, $15

EMANUEL DI PASQUALE, *Love Lines,* Vol. 88, Poetry and Italian American Studies, $10

JOSEPH ANTHONY LOGIUDICE AND MICHAEL CAROSONE, *Our Naked Lives: Essays from Gay Italian American Men,* Vol. 87, Gay Studies and Italian American Studies, $15

JAMES J. PERICONI, *Strangers in a Strange Land: A Survey of Italian-language American Books (1830–1945),* Vol. 86, Italian American Studies, $24

DANIELA GIOSEFFI, *Pioneering Italian American Culture: Escaping La Vita Cucina,* Vol. 85, Cultural Studies/ Women's Studies/Literary Arts, $22

MARIA FAMÀ, *Mystics in the Family,* Vol. 84, Poetry, $10

ROSSANA DEL ZIO, *From Bread and Tomatoes to Zuppa di Pesce "Ciambotto,"* Vol. 83, Italian American Studies, $15

LORENZO DELBOCA, *Polentoni,* Vol. 82, Italian Studies, $20

SAMUEL GHELLI, *A Reference Grammar,* Vol. 81, Italian American Studies, $20

ROSS TALARICO, *Sled Run,* Vol. 80, Fiction, $15

FRED MISURELLA, *Only Sons,* Vol. 79, Fiction, $17

FRANK LENTRICCHIA, *The Portable Lentricchia,* Vol. 78, Fiction, $17

RICHARD VETERE, *The Other Colors in a Snow Storm,* Vol. 77, Poetry, $10

GARIBALDI LAPOLLA, *Fire in the Flesh,* Vol. 76, Fiction, $25

GEORGE GUIDA, *The Pope Stories,* Vol. 75, Fiction, $15

ROBERT VISCUSI, *Ellis Island,* Vol. 74, Poetry, $28

ELENA GIANINI BELOTI, *The Bitter Taste of Strangers Bread,* Vol. 73, Fiction, $24

PINO APRILE, *Terroni,* Vol. 72, Italian American Studies, $20

EMANUEL DI PASQUALE, *Harvest,* Vol. 71, Poetry, $10

ROBERT ZWEIG, *Return to Naples,* Vol. 70, Memoir, $16

AIROS & CAPPELLI, *Guido,* Vol. 69, Italian American Studies, $12

FRED GARDAPHÉ, *Moustache Pete is Dead! Long Live Moustache Pete!,* Vol. 67, Literature/Oral History, $12

PAOLO RUFFILLI, *Dark Room/Camera oscura,* Vol. 66, Poetry, $11

VIA FOLIOS
A refereed book series dedicated to the culture of Italians and Italian Americans.

HELEN BAROLINI, *Crossing the Alps,* Vol. 65, Fiction, $14
COSMO FERRARA, *Profiles of Italian Americans,* Vol. 64, Italian American, $16
GIL FAGIANI, *Chianti in Connecticut,* Vol. 63, Poetry, $10
BASSETTI & D'ACQUINO, *Italic Lessons,* Vol. 62, Italian American Studies, $10
CAVALIERI & PASCARELLI, eds., *The Poet's Cookbook,* Vol. 61, Poetry/Recipes, $12
EMANUEL DI PASQUALE, *Siciliana,* Vol. 60, Poetry, $8
NATALIA COSTA, ed., *Bufalini,* Vol. 59, Poetry
RICHARD VETERE, *Baroque,* Vol. 58, Fiction
LEWIS TURCO, *La Famiglia/The Family,* Vol. 57, Memoir, $15
NICK JAMES MILETI, *The Unscrupulous,* Vol. 56, Humanities, $20
BASSETTI, ACCOLLA, D'AQUINO, *Italici: An Encounter with Piero Bassetti,* Vol. 55, Italian
     Studies, $8
GIOSE RIMANELLI, *The Three-legged One,* Vol. 54, Fiction, $15
CHARLES KLOPP, *Bele Antiche Stòrie,* Vol. 53, Criticism, $25
JOSEPH RICAPITO, *Second Wave,* Vol. 52, Poetry, $12
GARY MORMINO, *Italians in Florida,* Vol. 51, History, $15
GIANFRANCO ANGELUCCI, *Federico F.,* Vol. 50, Fiction, $15
ANTHONY VALERIO, *The Little Sailor,* Vol. 49, Memoir, $9
ROSS TALARICO, *The Reptilian Interludes,* Vol. 48, Poetry, $15
RACHEL GUIDO DE VRIES, *Teeny Tiny Tino's Fishing Story,* Vol. 47, Children's Lit, $6
EMANUEL DI PASQUALE, *Writing Anew,* Vol. 46, Poetry, $15
MARIA FAMÀ, *Looking For Cover,* Vol. 45, Poetry, $12
ANTHONY VALERIO, *Toni Cade Bambara's One Sicilian Night,* Vol. 44, Poetry, $10
EMANUEL CARNEVALI, Dennis Barone, ed., *Furnished Rooms,* Vol. 43, Poetry, $14
BRENT ADKINS, et al., ed., *Shifting Borders, Negotiating Places,* Vol. 42, Proceedings, $18
GEORGE GUIDA, *Low Italian,* Vol. 41, Poetry, $11
GARDAPHÈ, GIORDANO, TAMBURRI, *Introducing Italian Americana,* Vol. 40, Italian American
     Studies, $10
DANIELA GIOSEFFI, *Blood Autumn/Autunno di sangue,* Vol. 39, Poetry, $15/$25
FRED MISURELLA, *Lies to Live by,* Vol. 38, Stories, $15
STEVEN BELLUSCIO, *Constructing a Bibliography,* Vol. 37, Italian Americana, $15
ANTHONY J. TAMBURRI, ed., *Italian Cultural Studies 2002,* Vol. 36, Essays, $18
BEA TUSIANI, *con amore,* Vol. 35, Memoir, $19
FLAVIA BRIZIO-SKOV, ed., *Reconstructing Societies in the Aftermath of War,* Vol. 34, History, $30
TAMBURRI, et al., eds., *Italian Cultural Studies 2001,* Vol. 33, Essays, $18
ELIZABETH G. MESSINA, ed., *In Our Own Voices,* Vol. 32, Italian American Studies, $25
STANISLAO G. PUGLIESE, *Desperate Inscriptions,* Vol. 31, History, $12
HOSTERT & TAMBURRI, eds., *Screening Ethnicity,* Vol. 30, Italian American Culture, $25
G. PARATI & B. LAWTON, eds., *Italian Cultural Studies,* Vol. 29, Essays, $18
HELEN BAROLINI, *More Italian Hours,* Vol. 28, Fiction, $16
FRANCO NASI, ed., *Intorno alla Via Emilia,* Vol. 27, Culture, $16
ARTHUR L. CLEMENTS, *The Book of Madness & Love,* Vol. 26, Poetry, $10
JOHN CASEY, et al., *Imagining Humanity,* Vol. 25, Interdisciplinary Studies, $18
ROBERT LIMA, *Sardinia/Sardegna,* Vol. 24, Poetry, $10
DANIELA GIOSEFFI, *Going On,* Vol. 23, Poetry, $10
ROSS TALARICO, *The Journey Home,* Vol. 22, Poetry, $12
EMANUEL DI PASQUALE, *The Silver Lake Love Poems,* Vol. 21, Poetry, $7
JOSEPH TUSIANI, *Ethnicity,* Vol. 20, Poetry, $12

VIA Folios

A refereed book series dedicated to the culture of Italians and Italian Americans.

JENNIFER LAGIER, *Second Class Citizen,* Vol. 19, Poetry, $8

FELIX STEFANILE, *The Country of Absence,* Vol. 18, Poetry, $9

PHILIP CANNISTRARO, *Blackshirts,* Vol. 17, History, $12

LUIGI RUSTICHELLI, ed., *Seminario sul racconto,* Vol. 16, Narrative, $10

LEWIS TURCO, *Shaking the Family Tree,* Vol. 15, Memoirs, $9

LUIGI RUSTICHELLI, ed., *Seminario sulla drammaturgia,* Vol. 14, Theater/Essays, $10

FRED GARDAPHÈ, *Moustache Pete is Dead! Long Live Moustache Pete!,* Vol. 13, Oral Literature, $10

JONE GAILLARD CORSI, *Il libretto d'autore, 1860–1930,* Vol. 12, Criticism, $17

HELEN BAROLINI, *Chiaroscuro: Essays of Identity,* Vol. 11, Essays, $15

PICARAZZI & FEINSTEIN, eds., *An African Harlequin in Milan,* Vol. 10, Theater/Essays, $15

JOSEPH RICAPITO, *Florentine Streets & Other Poems,* Vol. 9, Poetry, $9

FRED MISURELLA, *Short Time,* Vol. 8, Novella, $7

NED CONDINI, *Quartettsatz,* Vol. 7, Poetry, $7

ANTHONY TAMBURRI, ed., *Fuori: Essays by Italian/American Lesbians and Gays,* Vol. 6, Essays, $10

ANTONIO GRAMSCI, P. Verdicchio, Trans. & Intro., *The Southern Question,* Vol. 5, Social Criticism, $5

DANIELA GIOSEFFI, *Word Wounds & Water Flowers,* Vol. 4, Poetry, $8

WILEY FEINSTEIN, *Humility's Deceit: Calvino Reading Ariosto Reading Calvino,* Vol. 3, Criticism, $10

PAOLO GIORDANO, ed., *Joseph Tusiani: Poet, Translator, Humanist,* Vol. 2, Criticism, $25

ROBERT VISCUSI, *Oration Upon the Most Recent Death of Christopher Columbus,* Vol. 1, Poetry, $3

Published by Bordighera, Inc., an independently owned, not-for-profit, scholarly organization that has no legal affiliation with the University of Central Florida and the John D. Calandra Italian American Institute, Queens College/CUNY.

www.ingramcontent.com/pod-product-compliance
Lightning Source LLC
LaVergne TN
LVHW041303080426
835510LV00009B/851